NEW ZEALAND

A SCENIC COLLECTION

WELDON
PUBLISHING

SYDNEY · HONG KONG · CHICAGO · LONDON

Distributed by Becket Sterling Ltd
28 Poland Road, Glenfield, Auckland

Published by Weldon Publishing New Zealand
A division of Weldon International Pty Ltd
1/372 Eastern Valley Way, Willoughby, NSW 2068, Australia

First published 1989
© Copyright Weldon International Pty Ltd

Editor: Alison Dench
Designer: Errol McLeary
Typeset in New Zealand by The Type Factory Ltd, Auckland
Printed in Hong Kong by Colorcraft Ltd

National Library of Australia Cataloguing-in-Publication Data:

Horne, Anna.
New Zealand, a scenic collection.

ISBN 1 86302 028 4.

1. New Zealand — Description and travel — 1981–   —
Views. 2. New Zealand — Description and travel —
1981–   . Joyce, Ray, 1947–   . II. Title.

993.103'7'0222

Imperceptibly, the constellation of the Southern Cross begins to fade. The night sky pales with hints of colour, the pastels of dawn. Aotearoa, New Zealand, first nation in the world to greet the day, lies waiting. Abruptly the sun is unleashed from the distant Pacific horizon and its brilliant rays set Mt Hikurangi, sacred mountain of the Raukumara Range, guardian of East Cape, ablaze.

Within minutes the startling light strikes the peaks of the other North Island sentinels — Ruapehu, Tongariro, Ngauruhoe, Taranaki — and the snow-capped heights of the Southern Alps, backbone of the South Island. It falls on the rolling hills of Otago and craggy Coromandel and awakens the gentle farmlands of Wairarapa and Waikato. It is this light, clear and intense, a light that some call harsh, that bestows on the New Zealand landscape a very special quality.

The day spreads quickly, for New Zealand is a slender land stretching from a subtropical 34°S to a subantarctic 47°S with less than 400 kilometres separating the coasts on the bulge of the North Island.

It is this long, narrow shape that determines the climate and so much of the landscape. Here we experience the maritime weather of an island, its patterns determined by the interaction of depressions rolling round the 'roaring forties' with highs generated over our nearest continental neighbours, Australia, beyond the Tasman Sea, and Antarctica, well to the south. Occasionally, cyclones descend from the tropics and the only other land masses within close range, the small islands of Fiji, Tonga, New Caledonia and the Cook Islands, 2000 kilometres away.

Befriended by this very isolation since breaking away from Gondwanaland millions of years ago, New Zealand has developed with an unmatched physical diversity and is, paradoxically, old and new at the same time. The classical beauty of the Southern Alps and the intricacies of the Marlborough Sounds and Fiordland, born of land — building processes long stilled by time, contrast dramatically with the volatile signs of earth under revision at the geothermal wildernesses of Rotorua and the smoking, active volcanoes on the Central Plateau.

In these pages you will find landscapes of mystery, views with no hints of human presence, and others where the raw shape of the countryside has been revealed by timber milling or enhanced by deciduous trees introduced from Europe; deserted beaches to dense rainforest, placid lakes to productive plains. In all corners of New Zealand fresh and unanticipated visual delights await you.

There is an old Maori proverb that says, Papatūānuku te matua o te tangata. Mother Earth is man's parent. This philosophy increasingly underlies New Zealanders' response to the environment and ensures that the natural heritage they are so proud of will survive.

Mighty Pacific swells create surf
at Cape Reinga in the far north.

Unrestrained beach and dune make way for orderly
farms on the coastal plains north-west of Kaitaia.

A freshwater loch nestled by hills at Waipapakauri,
just a stone's throw from the Tasman Sea.

The lonely miles of Pakiri Beach.

◁ North of Kaipara Harbour, the land patiently resists the Tasman surf.

The beauty of the huge dunes of South Head belies the treacherous nature of the entrance to Kaipara Harbour.

The carefully tended parkland of Wenderholm Regional Park borders the Waiwera River estuary.

If ever time stopped still, it was here by the peaceful Puhoi River.

The Auckland Harbour Bridge spans the narrowest channel of the extensive Waitemata Harbour, linking North Shore suburbs with the city centre.

The sheltered waters of the Firth of Thames are unruffled by a distant thunderstorm.

Turipeka Point silhouetted starkly against a stormy sky at day's end. ▷

◁ Sunlight accents form and colour as Colville hills fold into the bristling reeds of Umangawha Stream.

Craggy islets scoured by the sea out of sandstone cliffs are a feature of the Hahei coastline in Mercury Bay.

Completing the journey from its source at
Lake Taupo, over 300 kilometres to the south,
New Zealand's longest river, the Waikato,
divides into a myriad of small streams.

In the warm Bay of Plenty climate, intensive
agriculture has transformed the landscape into
a rural patchwork

The Whirinaki River meanders its last miles to
the sea through a valley of healthy mangroves.

One of East Cape's most dramatic landmarks, ▷
Gable End Foreland, dazzles the eye as early
morning sun strikes the escarpment.

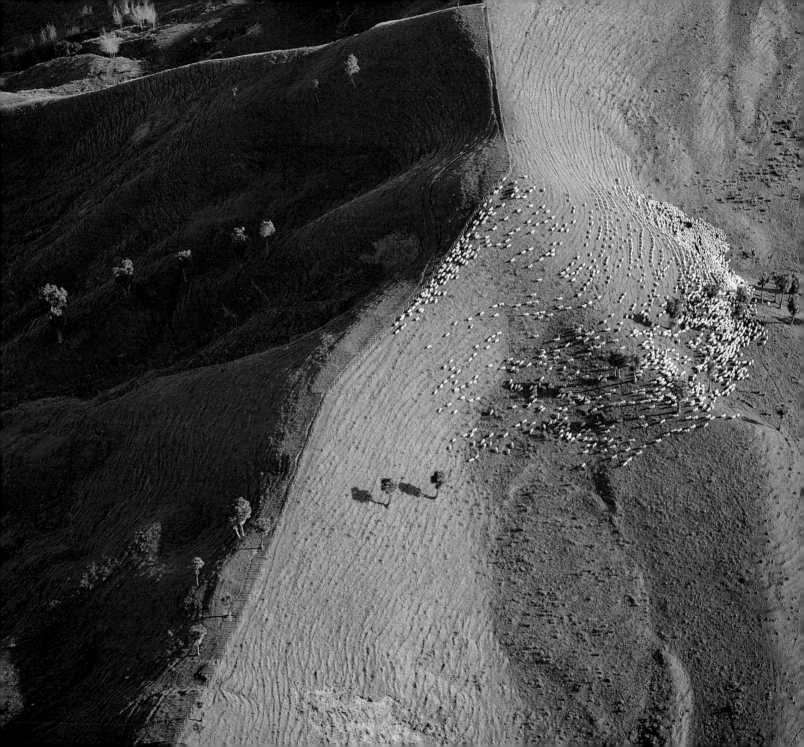

The rugged heights of the Raukumara Range, covered by impenetrable native forest, defy a blanket of mist.

◁ The hills at Tatapouri, their shape exposed by the clearance of the original bush cover, are modified further as sheep tracks terrace the slopes.

Grazing sheep and cabbage trees emerge from the mist at Mahia Peninsula.

Vegetation has barely taken hold on Mt ▷ Tarawera, which blew apart and scattered debris across the North Island in a violent eruption a hundred years ago.

The otherwise devastating earthquake at Napier in 1931 raised these valuable plains from the city's harbour.

A major fault line under the Rotorua region is responsible for the thermal activity that has made Whakarewarewa's Geyser Flat world famous.

There's an alien atmosphere here: the air is heavy with sulphurous gases and silica deposits form a strange landscape.

As the rising steam suggests, the Waimangu Cauldron series of lakes formed in craters left by the Tarawera eruption is constantly 'on the boil'.

Gifted to the nation by the Tuwharetoa Tribe in 1887, Mt. Ruapehu is the sacred centrepiece of New Zealand's first National Park.

Shadows darken the corrugations in the coastline at Omata, west of New Plymouth.

Gourmet cheeses are a product of north Okato, one of the many dairying districts around Taranaki.

Increasingly referred to by its Maori name of ▷ Taranaki, this isolated mountain, according to legend, once lived with the other volcanoes of the central North Island but was chased away to the coast after a feud with Tongariro.

The spindly remains of manuka trees strike
pose in a back corner of Wairarap

Many ships have foundered on the hostile reefs off Cape Palliser,
at the southern extremity of the North Island.

The tiny harbour created by a natural sea-wall at Castlepoint is the sole refuge for boats on the exposed Wairarapa coast.

Like cathedral spires,
the Putangirua Pinnacles
strike out for the sky.

The capital city, Wellington, displays its waterfront in a dazzle of light.

Throughout the intricate waterways of Queen Charlotte Sound placid inlets such as Shakespeare Bay abound.

The warmth of the sun is captured by the amphitheatre of hills behind a secluded beach in the Marlborough Sounds.

38

In an illusion of movement, solid limestone appears to flow forth from Takaka Hill, Nelson.

◁ Sunset is mirrored on the tidal flats of the sheltered Waimea Inlet.

Nelson's crystal-clear water, sunny unpolluted skies and a natural breakwater, albeit of boulders, not coral, are suggestive of Pacific islands closer to the tropics.

Toitū he kāinga, whatu ngarongaro he tangata. The land still remains ▷ when the people have disappeared.

42

Sunrise in autumnal Culverden.

Here on the Canterbury Plains the cycles of grain farming are shown by the changing textures of the orderly fields.

43

Pegasus Bay develops into a study in monochrome as thunderclouds darken the sky.

The French enclave of Akaroa nestles in the hills of Banks Peninsula.

Canterbury's acclaimed Lake Tekapo and the neighbouring Southern Alps don their winter attire as temperatures drop in early May.

Light and shadow highlight the Grampian Mountains and the vast basin of the Mackenzie Valley

ow cloud over bare South Canterbury hills evokes memories of English landscapes by Turner.

Above kahikatea forest on the Karangarua River flat, the foothills of the Southern Alps emerge briefly from low raincloud.

A moody light sets the haphazard piles of ▷ Punakaiki's Pancake Rocks in bold relief against the breakers.

In the Denniston bush, mosses camouflage a tangle of roots caught in the cycle of decay and regeneration.

50

The Fox and Franz Josef glaciers have their origins here in the freezing snow and ice of the Great Divide.

In an everchanging pattern the
Waitaki River constantly revises
the intricate braiding of its
course from the Alps to the Pacific.

Vibrant with the glowing colours
of autumn, Central Otago is at
its most alluring with the change
of season.

Maori lore explains that these unusual boulders on the beach at Moeraki were food baskets lost overboard from a voyaging canoe.

Cliffs make formidable boundaries to sheep paddocks south of Dunedin.

The seaward coast of the Otago Peninsula
between Taiaroa Head and Cape Saunders is a
unique breeding ground for wildlife —
albatrosses, sea-lions, penguins — from the
southern oceans.

It doesn't seem surprising that this 'Wild West' ▷
landscape at Flat Top Hill, Alexandra, saw its
share of gold seekers a hundred years ago.

Clear winter light captures a moment of stillness in the awesome fiord of Milford Sound.

Gracing the alpine skyline, the unblemished peaks of Fiordland stretch as far as the eye can see.

Proud bearers of natural heritage, the Kepler Mountains provide a sanctuary for a rare species of flightless bird, the takahe.

The Save Manapouri Campaign in the early 1970s marked an awakening amongst ▷
New Zealanders to their environment and ensured that the shoreline of this
unspoiled lake would never be disturbed by hydroelectric development.

The tantalising beauty of a cove near the entrance to Preservation Inlet is protected by its inaccessible location at the south-western extreme of the South Island.

A high altitude waterfall cascades from a basin of melted snow on Mt Burnett.

Where ice-age glaciers once ground their paths through ancient gneiss, mountains now meet sea at Doubtful Sound, Fiordland.